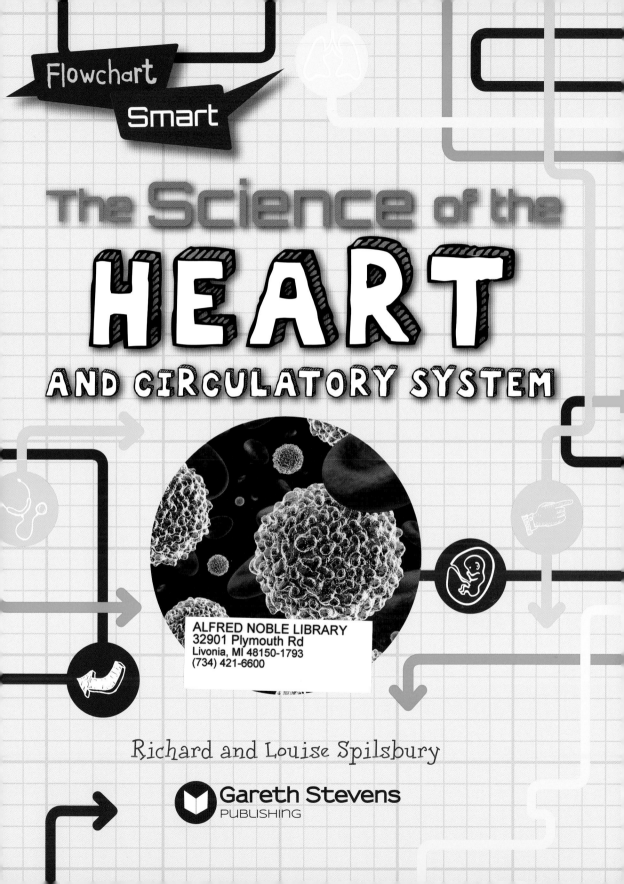

Flowchart Smart

The Science of the HEART AND CIRCULATORY SYSTEM

Richard and Louise Spilsbury

Gareth Stevens
PUBLISHING

MAR 1 7 2018

3 9082 13561 1476

Please visit our website, **www.garethstevens.com**.
For a free color catalog of all our high-quality books,
call toll free 1-800-542-2595 of fax 1-877-542-2596.

Cataloging-in-Publication Data
Names: Spilsbury, Richard.
Title: The science of the heart and circulatory system / Richard and Louise Spilsbury.
Description: New York : Gareth Stevens Publishing, 2018. | Series: Flowchart smart | Includes index.
Identifiers: ISBN 9781538207024 (pbk.) | ISBN 9781538206935 (library bound) | ISBN 9781538206836 (6 pack)
Subjects: LCSH: Heart--Juvenile literature. | Blood--Juvenile literature. | Cardiovascular system--Juvenile literature.
Classification: LCC QP111.6 S65 2018 | DDC 612.1--dc23

First Edition

Published in 2018 by
Gareth Stevens Publishing
111 East 14th Street, Suite 349
New York, NY 10003

Copyright © 2018 Gareth Stevens Publishing

Produced for Gareth Stevens by Calcium
Editors: Sarah Eason and Harriet McGregor
Designers: Paul Myerscough and Simon Borrough
Picture researcher: Rachel Blount

Cover art: Shutterstock: Denk Creative.

Picture credits: Shutterstock: Atm2003 12b, Tewan Banditrukkanka 36, Blend Images 4–5, BlueRingMedia 16, Busayamol
8–9, Gianni Caito 40–41, Designua 7r, Elenabsl 19, Fabiodevilla 34–35, Firma V 28–29, Juan Gaertner 26b, Garsya 8l,
Imtmphoto 6–7, Dmitry Kalinovsky 32–33, Sebastian Kaulitzki, 5, 21, 29br, Khuruzero 36–37, Lightspring 1, 15r, Magnia
30–31, Negovura 42–43, NoPainNoGain 10–11, Oculo 33r, Oorka 24–25, Lisa S. 34b, Ljupco Smokovski 14–15, Stihii
13, Syda Productions 26–27, John T Takai 39, Tefi 20, Wouter Tolenaars 18–19, Udra11 44bl, Vectorstockstoker 22,
Vetpathologist 24l, Tom Wang 44–45.

Printed in the United States of America
CPSIA compliance information: Batch #CS17GS: For further information contact Gareth Stevens, New York, New York at 1-800-542-2595.

Contents

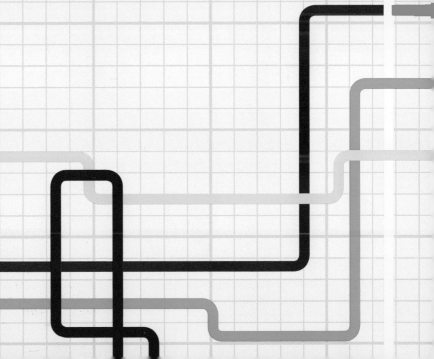

Chapter 1
The Human Heart

The human heart performs an incredible job. Every day, it pumps blood around the body through a network of tubes called **blood vessels**. It makes sure that **oxygen** reaches the **organs**, which allows them to work. It also ensures that waste from the body is carried away. The heart is the powerhouse of the entire human body.

The heart is the size of a grapefruit and it is located almost in the center of the chest, between the lungs. You can feel your heartbeat when you place your hand on the left side of your chest. This is because the heart is angled a little and a part of it taps against the left side of the chest as it beats. The heart is a vital organ. It is protected by the rib cage, the bones that form the chest.

When you exercise your heart pumps blood to your muscles.

The heart must beat every minute of every day to keep the body alive. The walls of the heart are made of a special kind of muscle called cardiac muscle. Unlike skeletal muscles, which pull on your bones to make body parts such as your arms and legs move, cardiac muscle does not get tired, even though it works all the time. It circulates the blood around the body three times every minute.

Get Smart!

Blood goes on an epic journey as it is pumped through the human body. There are 61,137 miles (100,000 km) of blood vessels in your body. If you laid them end-to-end, they would travel all the way around the world twice!

Blood vessels carry blood to the heart and carry blood away from the heart.

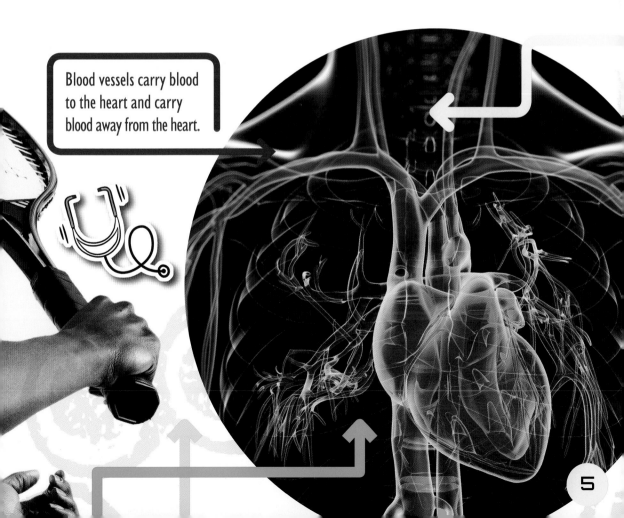

Parts of the Heart

The heart is usually described as a pump, but really it is like two pumps side by side. The heart is divided into two halves. Each half is divided into two blood-filled areas called chambers.

Each of the two chambers that make up the upper part of the heart is called an atrium. Together they are called the **atria**. The heart has a left atrium and a right atrium. The two chambers that form the lower part of the heart are called the left and right **ventricles**. There is also a thick layer of muscle called the septum running down the middle of the heart. It separates the left side and the right side of the heart.

First, the atria chambers fill with blood. They push that blood into the ventricles. Next the ventricles pump the blood out of the heart. At the same time as the ventricles squeeze the blood out of the heart, the atria refill with blood. **Valves** between the chambers keep blood from moving the wrong way.

Doctors listen to the heart using an instrument called a stethoscope.

Valves open up to let blood move from one chamber to another and close again to keep the blood from flowing backward. The mitral valve and the tricuspid valve let blood flow from the atria to the ventricles. The aortic valve and pulmonary valve control the flow of blood leaving the heart.

Get Smart!

The distinctive "lub-dub, lub-dub" sound of a heart is caused by the heart valves closing. The lub sound happens when the mitral and tricuspid valves close. The next dub sound happens when the aortic and pulmonary valves close after the blood has been squeezed out of the heart.

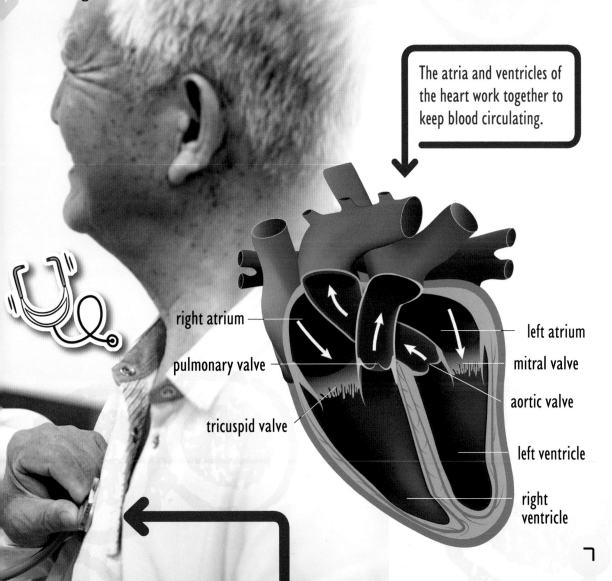

The atria and ventricles of the heart work together to keep blood circulating.

right atrium

pulmonary valve

tricuspid valve

left atrium

mitral valve

aortic valve

left ventricle

right ventricle

In a Heartbeat

The heart beats more than once every second, about 100,000 times every single day, and about 35 million times in a year. During an average human lifetime, a human heart beats more than 2.5 billion times. The human heart is one of the most hardworking organs in the body.

The heart beats, or pumps, by contracting, which is another word for tightening or squeezing. After the atria have filled with blood, the cardiac muscles contract to squirt the blood along. If you squeeze your hand into a fist, release, and then squeeze again you will get an idea of how the heart chambers contract to squirt out the blood. This is also about the same amount of force the heart muscles use to work. The difference is that the heart does this every second, even while you are resting or sleeping.

To measure how fast a heart beats people take their pulse rate. You can feel your pulse by lightly pressing two fingers on pulse points. These are the places you can see large blood vessels called **arteries** just beneath the skin. You should be able to feel a small throb beneath your fingers. This is the pulse and it is caused by the contractions of your heart creating waves of **pressure** along the arteries.

The walls of the heart squeeze its chambers to squeeze out blood just as we squeeze toothpaste out of a tube.

Take your pulse rate by resting your fingers on the side of your neck. Count the number of beats in 1 minute.

Get Smart!

A child's average heart, or pulse, rate when sitting is 90–120 beats per minute. As an adult, the pulse rate slows to an average of 72 beats per minute, when resting.

Get flowchart smart!

A Heartbeat

This flowchart shows what happens when a heart beats.

Blood enters the atria chambers of the heart.

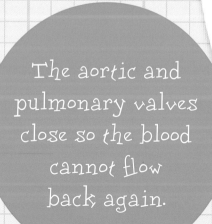

The aortic and pulmonary valves close so the blood cannot flow back again.

The atria contract, or squeeze, to force blood through valves into the ventricle chambers.

Once the blood has passed through, the mitral and tricuspid valves close. This keeps blood from flowing back into the atria.

The left and right ventricles contract and force the aortic and pulmonary valves open to squeeze blood out of the heart.

Flowchart Smart

Chapter 2

The Circulatory System

The movement of the blood through the heart and around the body through an intricate network of blood vessels is called the circulatory system. The heart is so efficient that it takes less than 1 minute to pump blood to every part of the body.

The blood in the circulatory system is on a loop. Blood enters the right side of the heart through large blood vessels, called the venae cavae. Then it is pumped through pulmonary arteries to the lungs. As the blood passes through the lungs it collects oxygen, which the body has breathed in from the air outside. Then this oxygen-rich blood is pumped back through the pulmonary **veins** to the left side of the heart.

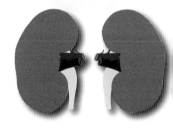

The heart then pumps the blood out through the aorta, the biggest artery in the body. The blood vessels that carry blood away from the heart are called arteries. They are the thickest blood vessels in the body because the pressure on the blood vessels is strongest at this point, when blood leaves the heart. The walls of the arteries contain muscles that contract, or squeeze and tighten, to keep the blood moving away from the heart.

The aorta, the largest artery in the body, is about the width of a garden hose.

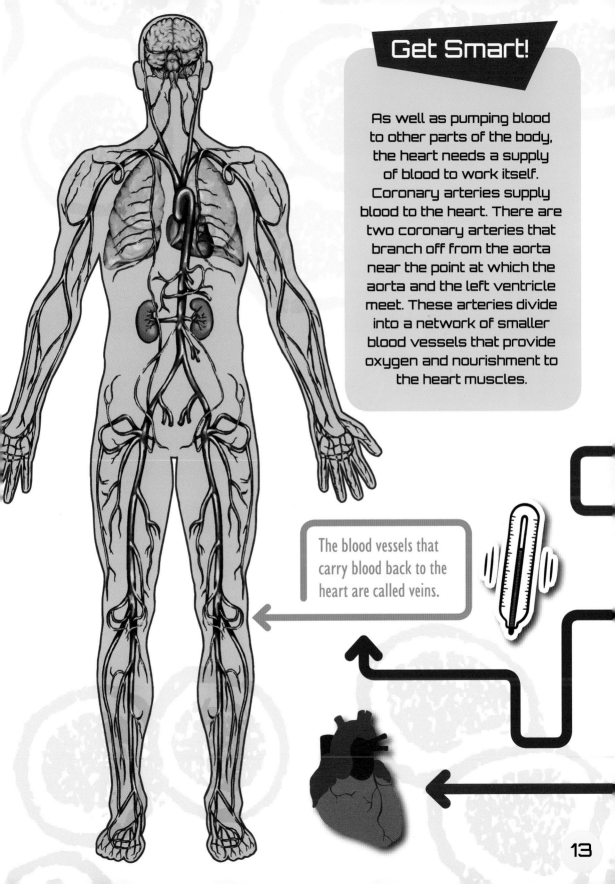

As well as pumping blood to other parts of the body, the heart needs a supply of blood to work itself. Coronary arteries supply blood to the heart. There are two coronary arteries that branch off from the aorta near the point at which the aorta and the left ventricle meet. These arteries divide into a network of smaller blood vessels that provide oxygen and nourishment to the heart muscles.

The blood vessels that carry blood back to the heart are called veins.

Into the Cells

After leaving the heart, oxygen-rich blood travels through the arteries and into smaller blood vessels called arterioles. From there it travels into blood vessels called **capillaries**. Capillaries are so narrow that 10 of them equal the thickness of a human hair. Even though they are tiny, capillaries are a very important part of the circulatory system. They deliver blood to the **cells**.

Get Smart!

Oxygen and **digested** food passes from the capillaries into cells by **diffusion**. Diffusion is when a substance moves from a region where it is in high concentration to a region where it is in low concentration. Capillaries have very thin walls so substances pass quickly and easily from them into cells. A huge length of capillaries surround and pass close to each cell, so there is a large **surface area** through which oxygen and dissolved food can pass.

Oxygen-rich blood travels around the body to help muscles work as a person exercises.

Cells make up all the different parts of the body. These red and white blood cells make up part of the blood along with **plasma** and **platelets**.

Capillaries reach individual cells so the bloodstream can deliver oxygen to them. Digested food from the **digestive system** is carried in the blood plasma. This also passes from the capillaries into the cells. The cells use oxygen to release **energy** from glucose, a type of sugar, in the dissolved food so they can live, work, and grow.

Capillaries connect the arteries with the veins. After delivering oxygen and dissolved food to the cells, blood moves back through capillaries to larger blood vessels called venules. Then it enters larger veins until it reaches the venae cavae and returns to the heart and lungs to collect fresh supplies of oxygen.

Get flowchart smart!

Blood Flow Around the Body

Let's look at how the heart pumps blood around the body once more, using a flowchart.

Blood is drawn into the right side of the heart.

Blood is pumped out of the right side of the heart through arteries to the lungs.

In the lungs, blood collects oxygen. It is then pumped back to the left side of the heart.

The heart pumps this oxygen-rich blood through the main artery, the aorta.

Blood travels all the way around the body.

Flowchart Smart

Chapter 3
Waste Disposal

We can think of the blood traveling from the heart as a fleet of delivery trucks carrying oxygen and food to the cells. When the cells combine oxygen with glucose to release energy, they make waste that must be removed. The bloodstream carrying the waste away from the cells is a little like the body's garbage truck!

When we exhale on a cold day we can see the water form droplets in the air.

When people combine fuel and oxygen to make electrical energy in a power plant, the waste that comes out of the power plant chimney is **carbon dioxide**, a type of gas. **Respiration** is the process in which cells combine oxygen and glucose to release energy, water, and waste substances such as carbon dioxide. Carbon dioxide can be poisonous if it builds up inside the body, so the cells must remove it.

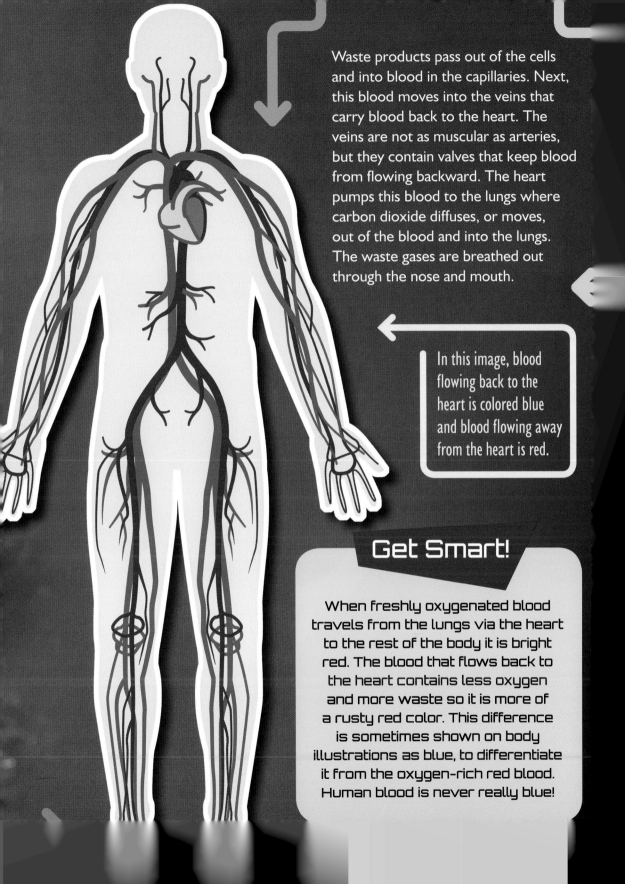

Waste products pass out of the cells and into blood in the capillaries. Next, this blood moves into the veins that carry blood back to the heart. The veins are not as muscular as arteries, but they contain valves that keep blood from flowing backward. The heart pumps this blood to the lungs where carbon dioxide diffuses, or moves, out of the blood and into the lungs. The waste gases are breathed out through the nose and mouth.

In this image, blood flowing back to the heart is colored blue and blood flowing away from the heart is red.

Get Smart!

When freshly oxygenated blood travels from the lungs via the heart to the rest of the body it is bright red. The blood that flows back to the heart contains less oxygen and more waste so it is more of a rusty red color. This difference is sometimes shown on body illustrations as blue, to differentiate it from the oxygen-rich red blood. Human blood is never really blue!

As blood circulates through the blood vessels it also passes through the kidneys. The kidneys are two bean-shaped organs located just below the rib cage, one on each side of the backbone. Each kidney is roughly the size of an adult fist. The kidneys are important because they remove waste and excess, or extra, fluid from the blood to keep it clean and healthy.

Each kidney consists of about one million filtering units called **nephrons**, so small they can only be seen with a high-powered microscope. Each nephron has a filter, called the glomerulus, and a tubule. The glomerulus allows fluid and waste products to pass through it, but not blood cells. The filtered fluid then moves through the tubule, which removes wastes from it and then sends any useful products, such as minerals, back to the blood. Some of the waste that the kidneys filter out of the blood comes from cell processes, such as excess water. Some waste is substances that your body does not need because it already has enough of them, like proteins.

The kidneys make urine (pee) from the excess fluid, waste, and other unwanted substances they filter from the blood. Urine flows down through narrow tubes called ureters to the bladder where it is stored until it gets full. Then the urine is passed out of the body through a tube called the urethra.

The kidneys are so important to our health that we have two of them, so we can survive if one gets injured or stops working.

The kidneys filter the blood up to 400 times a day. They filter 120 to 150 quarts (114 to 142 l) of blood to produce 1 to 2 quarts (1 to 2 l) of urine, which consists of wastes and extra fluid.

The kidneys are protected from injury by a large padding of fat, the lower ribs, and several muscles.

Get flowchart smart!

Waste Removal

This flowchart explains how the circulatory system removes waste from the body's cells.

During respiration, cells use oxygen and glucose to release energy. This creates a waste product called carbon dioxide.

The carbon dioxide passes up the throat and is exhaled through the nose and mouth.

The heart pumps the blood to the lungs where carbon dioxide diffuses out of the blood.

Carbon dioxide passes out of the cell and into the blood in the capillaries.

This blood contains little oxygen and some waste. It is now rusty red instead of bright red.

The blood travels from capillaries to veins and back to the heart.

Flowchart Smart

Chapter 4

Blood

An average adult has about 6 quarts (5.6 l) of blood in their body. Blood is mostly made up of yellowish fluid called plasma. This is the liquid part of the blood and it contains a lot of water. The plasma carries the other three most important parts of the blood: red blood cells, white blood cells, and platelets.

One drop of blood contains about five million red blood cells.

New blood cells are made in the **bone marrow**, the soft spongelike material found in the center of some bones.

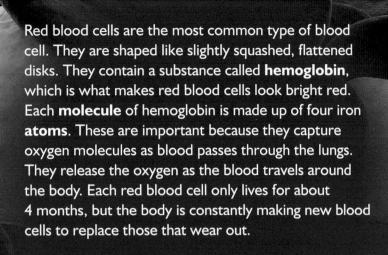

Red blood cells are the most common type of blood cell. They are shaped like slightly squashed, flattened disks. They contain a substance called **hemoglobin**, which is what makes red blood cells look bright red. Each **molecule** of hemoglobin is made up of four iron **atoms**. These are important because they capture oxygen molecules as blood passes through the lungs. They release the oxygen as the blood travels around the body. Each red blood cell only lives for about 4 months, but the body is constantly making new blood cells to replace those that wear out.

Most red and white blood cells are made by stem cells in the bone marrow. A baby's body has blood-cell producing bone marrow in all their bones. As people get older, the marrow in many of our bones stops working. As adults, blood cells are made in bones such as the ribs, parts of the humerus (upper arm bone), and femur (thigh bone).

Get Smart!

Everyone's blood belongs to one of four different groups, which are known by the letters: A, B, AB, and O. Each of the four different blood types can also either be "Rhesus positive" or "Rhesus negative" depending on whether or not it has a certain molecule on its cells. Do you know what blood type you have?

White Blood Cells

There are fewer white blood cells in the blood than red blood cells but they do a very important job. White blood cells defend the body against **infection** and keep us from getting harmful diseases. When the body fights an infection, it can make more white blood cells to battle the disease.

There are several types of white blood cells with different jobs. For example, imagine someone digs in dirt without wearing gloves. Then they eat their lunch without washing their hands. Bacteria from the ground enter their mouth and get into their bloodstream. Some of these bacteria can cause infections and disease. Lymphocytes are white blood cells that identify bacteria and other harmful body invaders, which we call **antigens**. The lymphocytes release special proteins called **antibodies**, which stick to the antigens.

When the antigens are labeled with antibodies, other white blood cells such as granulocytes can find and destroy them. After the white blood cells have learned to recognize and destroy a particular infection, lymphocytes will quickly attack the same bacteria if it enters the body again.

These lymphocytes are attacking a cancer cell.

The body makes more white blood cells when someone is sick to help him or her fight the infection.

Get Smart!

When yellow pus seeps from an infected wound, it looks pale because it is mostly made up of white blood cells. These are white blood cells that have worn themselves out defending the body against infection. White blood cells live from a few days to several months. Like red blood cells, they are constantly being replaced.

27

Blood Clots

When the skin is cut or damaged, blood leaks from the body's blood vessels. Blood loss is dangerous, so the body immediately works to close the gap. Platelets are like the blood's repair kit. They group together at wounds, helping the blood to clot, or set, and repair the damaged blood vessels.

Platelets are tiny oval-shaped cells. When a blood vessel breaks, platelets gather in the area and form a plug that stops the leak. They seal the wound by sticking both to the wound and to each other. They produce a stringy substance called fibrin. The fibrin forms a web that traps water and cells to form a clot.

Get Smart!

Anemia is a condition in which someone has fewer healthy red blood cells than normal. Anemia can be caused by blood loss or a lack of iron in the diet, and by certain diseases such as leukemia. People who are anemic may feel weak and tired and they may look paler than they usually do.

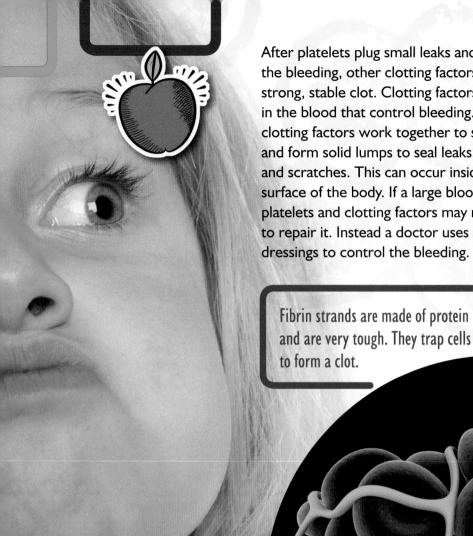

After platelets plug small leaks and stop or slow the bleeding, other clotting factors create a strong, stable clot. Clotting factors are proteins in the blood that control bleeding. Many different clotting factors work together to stop bleeding and form solid lumps to seal leaks, wounds, cuts, and scratches. This can occur inside and on the surface of the body. If a large blood vessel is cut, platelets and clotting factors may not be able to repair it. Instead a doctor uses sutures and dressings to control the bleeding.

Fibrin strands are made of protein and are very tough. They trap cells to form a clot.

This wound has been stitched to keep it closed. You can see where the clots of blood have dried and begun to harden into a scab.

Get flowchart smart!

Blood Vessel Repair

Follow the steps to see how blood heals damaged blood vessels.

When a person cuts him or herself, blood leaks from broken blood vessels.

Platelets in the blood flow to the wound and collect there to plug the gap. They release fibrin to keep more blood from escaping.

The clot hardens into a scab. This is a crusty covering that keeps more dirt and bacteria from entering the blood.

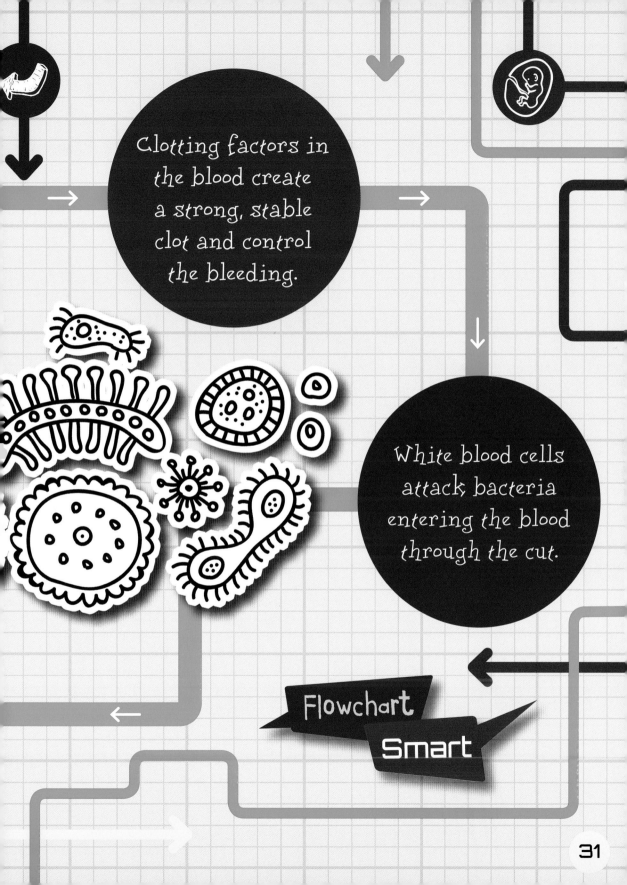

Clotting factors in the blood create a strong, stable clot and control the bleeding.

White blood cells attack bacteria entering the blood through the cut.

Flowchart Smart

Chapter 5

Heart and Circulation Problems

The first known person to have died from heart disease was a princess in ancient Egypt who died 3,500 years ago. Scientists have used modern scanning equipment to study her mummified body and they have discovered she had blocked arteries, a common problem today.

Sometimes people with blocked arteries need surgery to unblock them. The surgeons must reroute blood through other blood vessels to bypass the blockage.

Blocked coronary arteries cause heart attacks. A heart attack happens when the blood supply to the heart muscles is interrupted. The coronary artery supplies blood to the heart, and blockages form when fatty deposits build up inside it, restricting the flow of blood to the heart. Without fresh supplies of oxygen and fuel, the heart muscles cannot work. A heart attack can happen when a blood clot forms on the fatty deposits in the artery, or if a piece of the deposit breaks away and plugs the space inside the artery.

Circulation problems happen when deposits build up in other blood vessels too. The deposits narrow veins and capillaries and lead to poor circulation in other body parts like fingers and toes, or internal parts like the digestive system. In mild situations it can just cause a little discomfort. However, if it worsens it can affect vital organs and be very serious.

healthy artery

narrowed artery

blocked artery

Get Smart!

Have you ever sat awkwardly with your legs crossed for a long time until it feels like the limb has fallen asleep? By putting pressure on **nerves** and blood vessels you have prevented messages and blood flow from reaching the leg. The good news is that it soon returns to normal once you change position and the pressure is off.

When the body has a small wound or cut, the blood clots and the body repairs itself. If someone is in a major accident and loses a lot of blood, they will need a transfusion.

A transfusion is when a patient is given blood from a blood donor, someone who has donated their blood. It is vitally important that the correct type of blood is given to a patient and that the blood has been checked to be sure it does not contain any infections. If donated blood is infected in any way at all, it is destroyed. Donated blood is also tested for blood type to make sure it is compatible with the recipient's blood type.

People must only receive transfusions of the same type of blood as their own. This is because there are tiny antigens on the surface of the red blood cells. These antigens are proteins and sugars that the body uses to recognize other blood cells in the body. If blood containing "foreign" antigens enters the body, the patient's blood will reject the new blood. This is life threatening. Great care is taken by medical professionals to make sure this does not happen.

It does not hurt to give blood and it only takes the donor's body about two weeks to make new blood to replace that which they donated.

A blood transfusion can save a person's life after a serious accident in which they have sudden, heavy blood loss.

Get Smart!

When people donate blood, it can be separated into its different parts. This is so that people can not only receive whole-blood transfusions, but they can also be given transfusions of one of the parts of their blood that they lack, such as platelets, plasma, or red blood cells.

Helping the Heart

The study of the human heart and its disorders is known as cardiology. Cardiologists are doctors who use different machines to examine the human heart and help people with heart problems.

Electrical impulses make muscle cells contract and cause the heart to beat. An electrocardiogram (EKG) is a machine that measures the electricity in a patient's heart. Sensors attached to the skin detect the electrical signals produced by the heart each time it beats. It shows the signals as a line moving across a screen that occasionally spikes, or shoots upward. Cardiologists use information collected by the EKG to find out if a patient is having heart rhythm problems or even a heart attack.

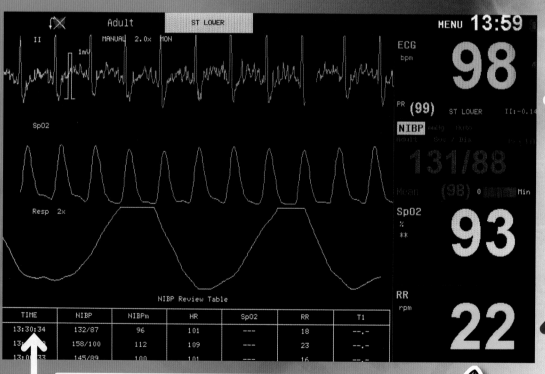

The green line is the readout from the EKG machine. An EKG is a quick, safe, and painless test.

Pacemakers have extended the lives of many thousands of people who have irregular heartbeats.

A pacemaker is a lifesaving machine that helps people with a weak or irregular heartbeat. A pacemaker is a small, battery-powered unit that is implanted inside a patient's body. Wires, called electrodes, are attached to the heart from this unit. The pacemaker delivers electrical pulses, which work like tiny electric shocks, and make the heart muscles contract and beat regularly again.

Get Smart!

Amazingly, in a few cases where someone has a very badly diseased heart, doctors carry out a heart transplant operation. They replace a failing heart with a healthy heart from a donor who has recently died. It is a risky operation that is only carried out on someone whose life is at great risk because their heart no longer works effectively.

Get flowchart smart!

How a Pacemaker Works

In this flowchart, see how a pacemaker keeps a person's heart beating regularly.

A pacemaker is implanted inside a patient's body, just above the rib cage.

The electrical pulses work like tiny electric shocks and make the heart muscles contract and beat regularly again.

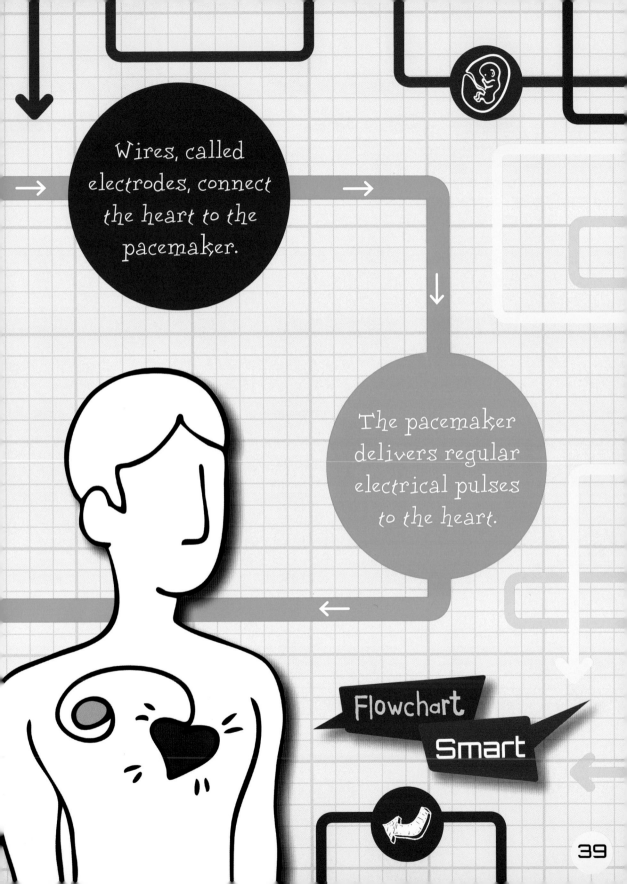

Wires, called electrodes, connect the heart to the pacemaker.

The pacemaker delivers regular electrical pulses to the heart.

Flowchart Smart

Chapter 6

Taking Care of Your Heart

To keep the body's heart and circulatory system healthy, people need regular exercise, a balanced diet, and medical care if any problems arise.

The heart is a muscle and like any muscle it must be exercised to become strong. Cardiovascular exercise such as swimming, dancing, or playing soccer makes you breathe harder and faster. When you exercise like this or run around a lot, your muscles need a lot more oxygen-filled blood.

To cope with the extra demands of exercise, the body temporarily directs blood flow away from areas that do not need it as much, such as the digestive system, and sends it toward the muscles instead. This increases the blood flow and therefore the amount of blood returning to the heart at any one time. When people exercise regularly, the left ventricle of the heart becomes bigger so it is ready to hold and release more blood at once. When each heartbeat delivers a bigger burst of blood, the heart does not have to contract quite as often. This reduces the amount of work it does and is why cardiovascular exercise helps your heart stay stronger for longer.

Get Smart!

When you run, you may have noticed feeling your heart pounding in your chest. That is because it is working harder. Try taking your pulse before and after a short period of exercise. What do you notice? Try to be active and get your heart working harder for at least 30 minutes every day if you can.

Tennis is a great sport for strengthening your heart.

Get flowchart smart!

Exercise and the Heart

This flowchart is a reminder of how exercise helps the heart.

A person runs around and begins to breathe harder and faster.

The muscles use the extra oxygen from the increased blood supply to make more energy.

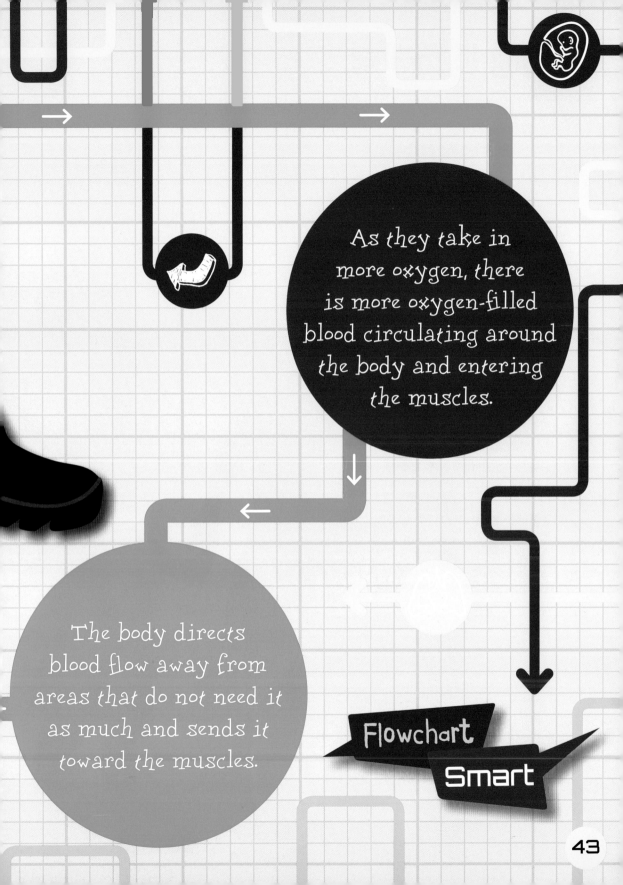

As they take in more oxygen, there is more oxygen-filled blood circulating around the body and entering the muscles.

The body directs blood flow away from areas that do not need it as much and sends it toward the muscles.

Flowchart Smart

Play It Safe

Eating a balanced, healthy diet is good for the whole body, including the heart and circulatory system. A healthy diet also helps prevent problems like blocked arteries and heart disease.

Foods that contain a lot of fat, like burgers, fries, potato chips, chocolate, and cake, should be eaten only occasionally and definitely not every day. These fatty foods can lead to clogged arteries.

Medical professionals recommend eating at least five servings of fruits and vegetables each day, and whole wheat bread, brown rice, whole wheat pasta, fish, and lean meat to help keep arteries clear. Smoking damages the heart and blood vessels, too. It damages the lining of the arteries, leading to a buildup of fatty material, which narrows the blood vessels and can increase the risk of a heart attack.

A balanced diet includes fruit, vegetables, and grains.

Get Smart!

When we eat more food than our body requires to make the energy it needs, the excess is stored as fat. These stores of fat can be used to release energy when the body needs it. The problem is that if people regularly eat more than they use, these fat stores build up and people become overweight. Being overweight puts a strain on the heart and can cause other health problems too.

The heart is an incredibly hardworking organ and the body's circulatory system is vital for our health and survival. Remember, the heart does more work than any other muscle in the body, so we should do all we can to take care of it, so it can go on looking after us!

Activity is fun, burns energy, and keeps your heart healthy.

Glossary

antibodies Substances produced by the body to fight disease.

antigens Substances that the body does not recognize and so tries to destroy.

arteries Blood vessels that carry blood away from the heart to the capillaries.

atoms The smallest particles of a substance that can exist by themselves.

atria Upper chambers of the heart where blood collects before passing to the ventricles.

blood vessels Tubes that carry blood around the body.

bone marrow Substance inside bones that makes new blood cells.

capillaries Tiny blood vessels that connect the arteries and veins.

carbon dioxide A gas in the air.

cells Very small parts that together form all living things.

diffusion When a substance moves from a region where it is in high concentration to a region where it is in low concentration.

digested Broken down so the body can use it.

digestive system Body parts that together break down food we eat so the body can use it.

energy The capacity to do work.

hemoglobin A protein that transports oxygen in the blood.

infection A disease caused by bacteria that enter the body.

molecule Tiny particle of a substance made from two or more atoms.

nephrons Tiny filtering structures in the two kidneys.

nerves Fibers that carry messages between the brain and the rest of the body.

organs Body parts like the heart or liver.

oxygen A gas in the air.

plasma The colorless fluid part of blood.

platelets Tiny cell fragments in blood that help stop bleeding when the body is injured.

pressure A pushing force.

respiration The process by which the body takes in oxygen and uses it to release energy from food.

surface area The total area of the surface of a 3-D object.

valves Flaps that close to keep blood from flowing in the wrong direction.

veins Blood vessels that carry blood from the capillaries to the heart.

ventricles The two main chambers of the heart, left and right.

For More Information

Books

Kenney, Karen Latchana. *Circulatory System* (Amazing Body Systems). Minneapolis, MN: Jump! Inc., 2017.

Leigh, Autumn. *The Circulatory System* (The Human Body). New York, NY: Gareth Stevens, 2012.

Mason, Paul. *Your Hardworking Heart and Spectacular Circulatory System* (Your Brilliant Body!). New York, NY: Crabtree Publishing Company, 2015.

Websites

Visit this website for fascinating heart facts:
www.coolkidfacts.com/facts-about-the-heart-for-kids

The blood and heart working together is also called the cardiovascular system—find out more at:
discoverykids.com/articles/your-cardiovascular-system

There is more to discover about the heart and circulatory system at:
kidshealth.org/en/kids/heart.html

Click through the links for lots of fun facts about the heart and blood at:
www.texasheart.org/ProjectHeart/Kids/Learn/fun_facts.cfm

Index